Isiah Thomas

by Mark Stewart

ACKNOWLEDGMENTS

The editors wish to thank Isiah Thomas for his cooperation in preparing this book.
Thanks also to Integrated Sports International for their assistance.

PHOTO CREDITS

All photos courtesy AP/Wide World Photos, Inc. except the following:

Brian Drake/Sports Chrome – cover
Isiah Thomas – 4 top left, 9, 12, 13, 24 top right, 36, 37, 46 top
Indiana University – 16 right, 24 bottom left

STAFF

Project Coordinator: John Sammis, Cronopio Publishing
Series Design Concept: The Sloan Group
Design and Electronic Page Makeup: Jaffe Enterprises, and
        Digital Communications Services, Inc.

LIBRARY OF CONGRESS CATALOGING-IN-PUBLICATION DATA
Stewart, Mark.
    Isiah Thomas / by Mark Stewart.
       p. cm. – (Grolier all-pro biographies)
    Includes index.
    Summary: Covers the personal life and basketball career of the star guard for the Detroit
Pistons.
    ISBN 0-516-20153-0 (lib. binding)–ISBN 0-516-26004-9 (pbk.)
    1. Thomas, Isiah, 1961– –Juvenile literature. 2. Basketball players–United States–
Biography–Juvenile literature. 3. Detroit Pistons (Basketball team)–Juvenile literature.
(1. Thomas, Isiah, 1961– . 2. Basketball players. 3. Afro-Americans–Biography.)
I. Title. II. Series.
GV884.TG47S84 1996
796.332'092–dc20
[B]   96-33791
                                                                                          CIP
                                                                                          AC

Grolier **ALL-PRO** *Biographies*™

Isiah Thomas

by
Mark Stewart

CHILDREN'S PRESS®
A Division of Grolier Publishing
New York • London • Hong Kong • Sydney
Danbury, Connecticut

Contents

Who

Am I?

In basketball, every team needs someone who can come through when the odds are long and time is running short. For fifteen years in college and the pros, my teammates looked for me to be that kind of person. Maybe it's because I was used to that role. As the youngest child in my family, I was our last chance at a better life. If I didn't make it, we would all have run out of time. My name is Isiah Thomas, and this is my story . . . "

"Every team needs someone who can come through when the odds are long."

Growing Up

Isiah Thomas was the youngest child born to a struggling family on the West Side of Chicago. The toughest part of Isiah's childhood was that his father left home and his mother had to raise nine children on her own. During the 1950s, Isiah's father had become the first African-American foreman for International Harvester, a company that makes farm equipment. But in the 1960s, he lost his job and could not find another company willing to hire a black man for a similar position. Frustrated and depressed, Isiah's father abandoned his family. Isiah remembers, "My father was a very, very intelligent man. He was frustrated because he wasn't allowed to use his intelligence."

So it was up to Isiah's mother, Mary, to hold the family together. Mary Thomas encouraged her seven sons to play sports as a way of keeping them away from drugs, crime, and gangs. But one at a time, the oldest Thomas boys drifted into the life of the streets.

Isiah with his mother, Mary Thomas, who encouraged him to play sports as a way to avoid trouble

Isiah still remembers these difficult times and how his brothers' mistakes affected him. "My family moved a lot when I was young. Often, we would live in a house with only three bedrooms for the ten of us. We always lived in a tough neighborhood—gangs, crime, drugs, and alcohol were all around me. Some of my older brothers got caught up in it, but fortunately I was able to learn from their mistakes. They experienced every bad experience for me."

Isiah attended Our Lady of Sorrows Elementary School, which was next to the church where his mother worked. Mary walked Isiah to school just about every morning, and she was involved in many of Isiah's after-school activities. Isiah was a good student. His favorite subject was math. He knew how to figure decimals long before his classmates did because he connected math to his favorite sport—basketball. He knew how to figure his basketball scoring and assist averages, and this helped him understand math problems in the classroom. Isiah's least favorite subject was history. Isiah was frustrated because his school's history books contained little about the achievements and contributions of African-Americans.

As so many of his older brothers had turned to gangs and drugs, little Isiah was Mary's last hope for happiness. Mary believed that if she could keep Isiah focused on school and sports, he could use his basketball skills to get a decent education and a good job. She hoped Isiah would help the family escape to a better life.

Mary had good reason to hope. At the age of three, Isiah could dribble a basketball so well that he put on halftime exhibitions at local youth league games. Over the years, he got better and better, sharpening his shooting, dribbling, and defensive skills against some of the city's best players in nearby Gladys Park. In eighth grade, Isiah tried to win a scholarship to Weber High School, but the coach rejected him because, at 5'8", he was too small. Luckily, a man named Gene Pignatore

When Isiah was a teenager, he and his friend Mark Aguirre (left) would roam the streets of Chicago looking for a pickup basketball game. In 1981, they were the first two players chosen in the NBA draft, and they eventually became teammates on the Detroit Pistons.

watched him play and saw a lot of talent within Isiah's skinny body.

Pignatore was the basketball coach at St. Joseph's School in suburban Chicago. He thought Isiah had the look of a winner and offered him a scholarship. Coach Pignatore warned Isiah that his schoolwork would be demanding, and that he would have to wake up at sunrise each morning to make the long train ride to school. Isiah accepted the challenge and enrolled at St. Joseph's in the ninth grade.

Isiah's first day at St. Joseph's was incredible. He gazed out the train window as the slums of the West Side slowly gave way to the green lawns and parks of the Chicago suburbs. When he walked up the stairs and down the hallways of St. Joseph's, he saw confident kids and happy smiles. This was where Isiah wanted to be, and he decided that nothing would keep him from making the most of this opportunity.

At first, Isiah found it difficult to keep up with his schoolwork. But he studied harder than he ever had in his life and eventually blossomed into an honors student. And, as he grew to over six feet tall, he also became a terrific basketball player. "Basketball actually helped me to balance my time," Isiah remembers. "With practices and games after school, I knew I had a specific

At St. Joseph's High School, Isiah made All-State and won a scholarship to Indiana University.

amount of time for studying. So sports gave me a schedule to go by. That, in turn, helped me to learn self-discipline. I believe that school teaches you how to discipline yourself and how to be organized. Of course, these skills won't get you very far if you don't become a good reader. Being able to read is extremely important for functioning in today's society."

A high-school portrait of Isiah

Isiah soon became known as one of the best high-school basketball players in Chicago. Other teams designed their defenses to cover Isiah closely, but he managed to beat them almost every time. If he was double- or triple-teamed, Isiah somehow found an open shot or delivered a perfect pass. In his junior year, he led St. Joseph's to a second-place finish at the Illinois state championships. As a senior, he was honored as a high-school All-American and was recruited by the country's top colleges. Isiah chose to attend Indiana University, where he would play under coach Bobby Knight.

College

Isiah Thomas used a combination of brains and basketball to get himself out of the ghetto and into one of the Midwest's finest universities. How he performed at Indiana University would determine whether the rest of the Thomas family would escape from poverty. Isiah felt that pressure on the campus and in the classroom. But it was nothing compared to the pressure he felt on the basketball court.

Indiana basketball coach Bobby Knight regularly screamed at his players and seemed to enjoy humiliating them in front of thousands of people. Isiah could not believe some of the things that Coach Knight said. Isiah often stood up for his teammates when he felt Knight had gone too far. This resulted in a tense relationship between the fiery coach and his young point guard.

Isiah knew that Knight was a great coach and a tremendous leader, but he found it hard to accept some of Knight's behavior. Once, during a nationally televised game Knight grabbed Isiah by his jersey and started screaming at him. Even when the

Years

Coach Knight yells instructions to his star.

Hoosiers were winning, Isiah was not happy.

In Isiah's second season, he guided the Indiana Hoosiers to its second straight Big 10 Conference title. He led the team in scoring and assists and earned All-America honors for his inspiring play. It was a rare honor for a sophomore. In the NCAA tournament, Isiah caught fire and led the Hoosiers to the national championship. He scored 23 points in the championship game and was named Final Four Most Outstanding Player. In just two years, he had done everything a college player could possibly do. He knew a

Above: Isiah cuts the net after Indiana defeated North Carolina University in the 1981 NCAA championship game. In just two years at Indiana, Isiah became one of the top basketball players in the nation.

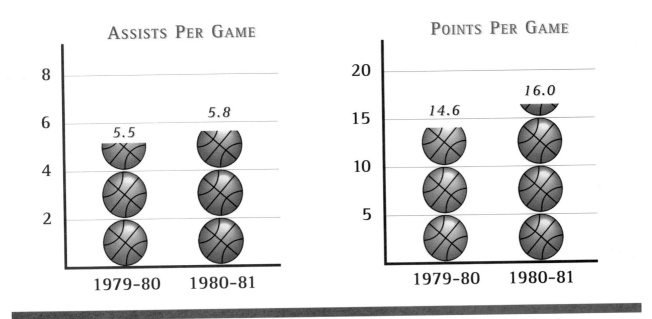

ASSISTS PER GAME

8
6   5.8
     5.5
4
2

1979–80   1980–81

POINTS PER GAME

20
                  16.0
15   14.6
10
5

1979–80   1980–81

high-paying job awaited him in the NBA, and he dreaded the prospect of playing another season for Bobby Knight. So Isiah decided to leave school and turn pro.

Although Isiah was just 20 years old when he ended his college career, he had little left to prove. "I could have waited a couple of years [to enter the NBA], but could my family have waited? My mother had sacrificed so much for me, more than I'll ever know. I wanted to give something back to her."

Isiah is one of only three Indiana players to earn All-America honors in the 1980s and 1990s. The most recent Hoosier All-American was Calbert Cheaney, who now plays in the NBA.

The Story

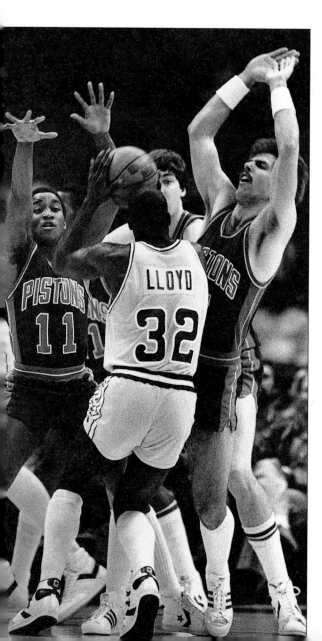

Isiah Thomas was selected by the Detroit Pistons with the second pick in the 1981 NBA draft. The Pistons were a team looking for answers, and they found one in Isiah. He took over the point-guard role, where he fed the ball to scorers John Long and Kelly Tripucka, who averaged over 20 points each. By midseason, the Pistons were a .500 team. Isiah was being hailed as the second-best point guard in the league behind the legendary Magic Johnson. Fans loved Isiah's crisp passes, stylish play, and radiant smile. He won a starting spot in the All-Star Game, a rare honor for a rookie.

Isiah (left) and Kelly Tripucka (right) stop Golden State's Louis Lloyd.

Continues

In the late 1980s, the Detroit Pistons had many stars, but Isiah was the team's superstar.

Within a few seasons, Detroit had assembled a squad of tough, hungry players such as Bill Laimbeer, Joe Dumars, and Dennis Rodman. With Isiah leading the way, the Pistons made a run at the title in the 1988 playoffs. They beat Michael Jordan and the Chicago Bulls, and then shocked the Boston Celtics to reach the NBA Finals. There, the Pistons met the Los Angeles Lakers, the defending NBA champions.

After Isiah joined the team, the Pistons acquired two more tough and gritty players—Dennis Rodman (left) and Bill Laimbeer (right).

In the Finals, the Pistons were up 3 games to 2 against the Lakers. In Game Six, Isiah went wild, scoring a record 25 points in the third quarter alone. But the Lakers came back to win 103–102, and they won Game Seven two days later to steal the crown back from the Pistons.

Although he injured his ankle in the series, Isiah continued to play well in the 1988 NBA Finals.

Isiah was heartbroken after losing in 1988, but a year later Detroit was back in the Finals. This time the Pistons swept Los Angeles in four straight games to win the 1989 NBA championship. In 1990, Isiah led Detroit to the Finals again, against the Portland Trailblazers. After an overtime loss in Game Two, Isiah took

After losing to Los Angeles in 1988, the Pistons beat the Lakers in the 1989 NBA Finals.

Winning the NBA championship was an emotional moment for Isiah.

control and buried the Blazers. Portland's Clyde Drexler and Terry Porter were helpless against Isiah's slashing drives and pull-up jumpers, and he picked the Blazers apart with his pinpoint passes. Without much trouble, the Pistons won their second straight NBA title, and Isiah was named MVP of the Finals.

Isiah's final season as a player was 1993–94. Slowed by injuries, he was still putting up big numbers when an Achilles tendon injury ended his career. Today, he is the executive vice president and part owner of the Toronto Raptors.

Portland can't stop a slashing drive by Isiah, who led the Pistons to their second straight NBA championship in 1990.

Timeline

1975: Enrolls at St. Joseph's High School

1984: Named MVP of NBA All-Star Game

1979: Accepts a scholarship from Indiana University

1981: Leads the Indiana Hoosiers to the NCAA basketball championship

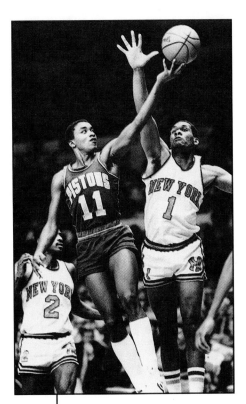

1985: Sets an NBA record with 1,123 assists for the Detroit Pistons

1994: Retires as a player and takes a front-office position with the expansion Toronto Raptors

1990: Leads Detroit to its second straight NBA title and is named MVP of the NBA Finals

Game

 siah and good friend Magic Johnson caused a sensation when they gave each other a center-court kiss prior to a Lakers-Pistons game.

I n 1988, Isiah tied an NBA Finals record with six steals in a game against the Lakers.

Action!

Isiah made the 1980 Olympic team and was ready to go for the gold. But the United States boycotted the Olympic Games that year for political reasons, and Isiah had to stay home.

"My most satisfying moment was when we won back-to-back NBA championships."

Isiah created opportunities for teammates by taking the ball to the hoop and then dishing off when he was double-teamed.

"Vision and court awareness were the two biggest things I brought to my position."

Dealing

Isiah's final season as a player was 1993–94. He was still putting up big numbers when an Achilles tendon injury ended his career. But this was hardly the end of Isiah's basketball life. A few months later, the Toronto Raptors announced that Isiah had agreed to become part owner of the team and run its basketball operations. The Raptors were an NBA expansion franchise scheduled to begin playing in 1995. When Isiah arrived, there were no players under contract, and the team had not yet selected a coach. It would be up to Isiah to bring together a brand-new NBA team.

No one could think of a better man for the job. Isiah had already proven that he could mold a group of players into a winning team. He also understood the business of basketball because he had been president of the players' union. Isiah was not the first NBA superstar to go directly from the hardwood

With It

to the front office, nor was he the first African-American to assume such a powerful role in an NBA organization. But he was the first former player—black or white—ever to be entrusted with the awesome responsibility of assembling a pro team from scratch.

In 1995, Isiah was introduced as vice president of the new Toronto Raptors basketball team.

How Did

Trapped by Harvey Grant and Tom Gugliotta of the Washington Bullets, Isiah looks to pass to a teammate.

He Do It?

Isiah Thomas studied videotape for hours each week to improve his play. Was he looking at opponents? No. He was watching teammates. By knowing all the little details about his fellow Pistons he could get them the ball when they could do the most with it.

"I had to know every single thing about our basketball team . . . everything about each player."

The Grind

Isiah gets a hug from his mother after winning the
MVP award in the 1986 All-Star Game.

Isiah presents a Pistons jersey to President George Bush after winning the NBA championship in 1990.

Isiah Thomas knows that being an NBA superstar did not make him any better or any worse than anyone else. But he says that remembering that can be a real challenge when everyone tells you how great you are all the time.

"The most difficult thing about being a professional athlete is being able to separate the image that you become from the person that you are. It is always important to remember who you are and where you came from."

Isiah's son, Joshua, celebrates Christmas with Isiah's mother, Mary Thomas.

Isiah Thomas is married and has two children. His wife's name is Lynn, and his kids are Joshua and Lauren. "During the off-season," he says, "I really enjoy spending time with my wife and children."

Isiah was his family's only chance of escaping the ghetto. When it became clear that he was a potential star, the family met and discussed a long-term plan. When Isiah strayed from the plan, his brothers would remind him of his responsibilities.

Matters

Isiah greets his relatives outside the locker room after another Detroit victory.

"I would sit down and take all the criticism, but I realize now that it helped me as a person."

Say What?

What do basketball people say about Isiah Thomas?

"He's a spontaneous, creative player who makes things happen."

–*Pat Riley, Miami Heat head coach*

"The greatest physical quality about him was his eyes. He had tremendous vision."

–*Bobby Knight,*
Indiana University coach

"I love watching my buddy Isiah dribbling the basketball."

–*Magic Johnson,*
  Los Angeles Lakers great

"He can put up a three-pointer on you, he can drive by you, he can pull up and hit the jumper, or he can hit somebody with a pass for an easy basket."

–*Cedric Maxwell, former Boston Celtics forward*

"There wasn't anything Isiah couldn't do—or didn't do—on the basketball court."

–*Don Nelson, longtime NBA coach*

"He makes sure everybody is involved."

–*Bill Laimbeer, former teammate*

Career

Isiah proved himself a true "double threat" in 1984–85, when he became the only player in NBA history to record more than 1,000 assists and average over 20 points a game in the same season.

Isiah was a member of the NBA All-Rookie team in 1982. He was a first-team All-NBA selection from 1984 to 1986.

Isiah pretends to defend against Nate Archibald (7) during an All-Star Game warm-up.

Highlights

Isiah is one of the most respected men in basketball. In 1987, he won the league's citizenship award for his community work, and in 1990, he won the NBA Finals MVP trophy.

Isiah became the Detroit Piston's all-time scoring leader in 1991. He also holds the team record for career assists.

Isiah played in the All-Star Game in every season except his last. He holds the all-time record for career steals in All-Star play, with 31.

In a 13-year career, Isiah was perhaps the most popular Detroit Piston of all time. When he retired, Detroit fans were sorry to see him go.

Reaching

Miami Dolphins head coach Jimmy Johnson, Isiah, former Dolphins linebacker Nick Buoniconti, and Nick's son Marc (seated) work to raise funds for the Miami Project to Cure Paralysis. Marc suffered a paralyzing injury in a college football game.

Out

Isiah signs autographs at a dinner to benefit the Association for the Help of Retarded Children.

I siah Thomas didn't mind being a role model for kids when he played, and he still enjoys spending time with them. Prior to the 1995 season, he took 40 children from the Toronto area to a local amusement park and everyone had a blast!

Isiah took the problem of crime in Detroit very seriously when he played there. In 1986, he approached Mayor Coleman Young and offered to head a campaign called No Crime Day. It had worked in his native Chicago, and Isiah thought it might work in Detroit, too. The program was a success, thanks largely to Isiah's hard work.

"It was basically a consciousness-raising effort to let the community know that if you become involved, we can do something to stop this problem."

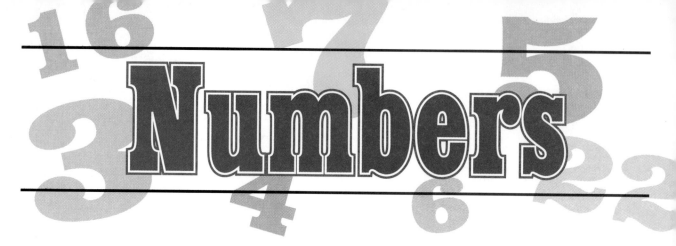

Numbers

Name: Isiah Lord Thomas III

Nickname: Zeke

Born: April 30, 1961

Height: 6' 1" **Weight:** 180 pounds

Uniform Number: 11

College: Indiana University

I siah's value becomes clear when you consider that an assist is given when a pass leads directly to a basket. That means he "created" more than 37 points per game with his passing and shooting.

Year	Team	Games	Assists	Assists Per Game	Points	Points Per Game
1981–82	Detroit Pistons	72	565	7.8	1,225	17.0
1982–83	Detroit Pistons	81	634	7.8	1,854	22.9
1983–84	Detroit Pistons	82	914*	11.1	1,748	21.3
1984–85	Detroit Pistons	81	1,123*	13.9*	1,720	21.2
1985–86	Detroit Pistons	77	830	10.8	1,609	20.9
1986–87	Detroit Pistons	81	813	10.0	1,671	20.6
1987–88	Detroit Pistons	81	678	8.4	1,577	19.5
1988–89	Detroit Pistons	80	663	8.3	1,458	18.2
1989–90	Detroit Pistons	81	765	9.4	1,492	18.4
1990–91	Detroit Pistons	48	446	9.3	776	16.2
1991–92	Detroit Pistons	78	560	7.2	1,445	18.5
1992–93	Detroit Pistons	79	671	8.5	1,391	17.6
1993–94	Detroit Pistons	58	399	6.9	856	14.8
Totals		979	9,061	9.3	18,822	19.2

* Led League

What If...

Every kid dreams of being an NBA star, but the odds against it are extremely high. As far as I was concerned, once I received an athletic scholarship to college I had 'made it.' I knew that if something happened to keep me from pursuing a basketball career, I had the means to succeed in life off the court. Actually, had I not played in the NBA, I would probably be working in the court—as a lawyer. After leaving school early, I went back and finished my degree in criminal justice. I had to. . . I had promised my mother and that was a promise she wasn't about to let me break!"

Glossary

DECENT proper and
respectable

DISCIPLINE to teach good
behavior, often using rewards
and punishment

FUNCTION the reason for
using a person or object; use

HUMILIATE to embarrass

APPROACH to ask a person to
perform a task or favor

BLOSSOMED grew

CONFIDENT feeling trust and
belief in oneself

CONTROVERSY a disagreement;
an argument

RETIRE to stop working at a job

SCHOLARSHIP money given to a student to help pay for school

SELF-DISCIPLINE the ability to train oneself to exercise proper behavior

SPEARHEAD to serve as leader; to motivate or inspire others

SPECIFIC focused on one particular thought or object

SPONTANEOUS free to use one's natural ability; not planned or forced

LURK to hide close by, ready and waiting to appear

PHENOMENAL extraordinary; remarkable

POTENTIAL the ability to grow or change

PROSPECT something that is looked forward to and expected

RADIANT shining brightly; beaming

RECRUITED asked to join a team or organization

Index

About The Author

Mark Stewart grew up in New York City in the 1960s and 1970s—when the Mets, Jets, and Knicks all had championship teams. As a child, Mark read everything about sports he could lay his hands on. Today, he is one of the busiest sportswriters around. Since 1990, he has written close to 500 sports stories for kids, including profiles on more than 200 athletes, past and present. A graduate of Duke University, Mark served as senior editor of *Racquet*, a national tennis magazine, and was managing editor of *Super News*, a sporting goods industry newspaper. He is the author of every Grolier All-Pro Biography.